5OTH Anniversary Edition

Genuine Autographed Collectible

Wee Willie Winkie

Gift Card

Date:

To:

From:

Message:

Timeless Classic, Children's Literature, Pets, Dogs, Education, Elementary School

Wee Willie Returns Never Give Up! Never Lose Hope! A True Story!

©1970 First Edition, @2022, By Jacqueline Malman. All Rights Reserved.

ISBN Hardcover: 978-1-885872-87-6
ISBN E-Book: 978-1-885872-86-9
Library of Congress Catalog Card Number: 2022905657

Author Fan Mail: WeeWillie@PalmBeachBookPublisher.com

Palm Beach Book Publisher books may be purchased for education,
business, or sales promotional use.
Website: www.PalmBeachBookPublisher.com
Email: Sharon@PalmBeachBookPublisher.com
Phone: 917-767-5843

Cover and Interior Book Design: Creative Genius Sharon Esther Lampert
Website: www.SharonEstherLampert.com
Email: Sharon@SharonEstherLampert.com

To Order Book:
Ingram, 1 Ingram Blvd. La Vergne, TN 37086-3629
Phone: 615-793-5000
Fax orders: 615-287-6990

First Edition

Manufactured in the United States of America

50TH Anniversary Edition

Wee Willie Returns

Never Give Up! Never Lose Hope! A True Story!

Jacqueline Malman
Author & Illustrator

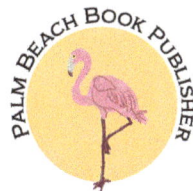

Palm Beach Book Publisher
Florida

What Do Books Do?

BOOKS ARE POWERFUL!

Books Educate!
Books Enlighten!
Books Empower!
Books Entertain!
Books Emancipate!
Books Spring Eternal!
Books Drive Exploration!
Books Spark Evolution!
Books Ignite Revolution!

Sharon Esther Lampert

To my favorite children,
Stanford and **E**lizabeth

Rave Book Reviews

"The lesson of hope learned in this book will last a lifetime!
Losing a beloved pet and finding your pet even if it takes
days, months, or even years is a JOY to behold!"
— Eve Paikoff, Parent

"I taught kindergarten class for 30 years.
This is a good character-building children's book.
The earlier kids learn the life lessons of never giving up
and never losing hope the better. BRAVA!"
— Esther Tulkoff, Teacher

As a teacher, mother and new grandmother,
I want all my kids to learn the lessons in this wonderful book.
I love my dog dearly, and his companionship is a gift of
unconditional love that I cherish. I am delighted to join
in the celebration of the 50TH Anniversary Edition!
— Elaina Merlis, Teacher

This is Wee Willie Winkie.

-1-

Wee Willie lives with Stanford and Elizabeth.
They take good care of him.
They wash and brush him every day.

Wee Willie eats small pieces of food from a small dish. He sleeps in a small bed.

Wee Willie wears a small coat on cold days.

One day, the children could not find
Wee Willie. They looked near his brush.
They looked near his small dish and small bed.

They looked near his small coat. They looked in every small place. **Wee Willie** was lost.

They looked inside and outside.
But, Wee Willie was lost.
Stanford wept, "Wee Willie is lost!"
Elizabeth wept, "Wee Willie is lost!"

The children told Mother, "Wee Willie is lost!
Please help us find Wee Willie. Please, please!"

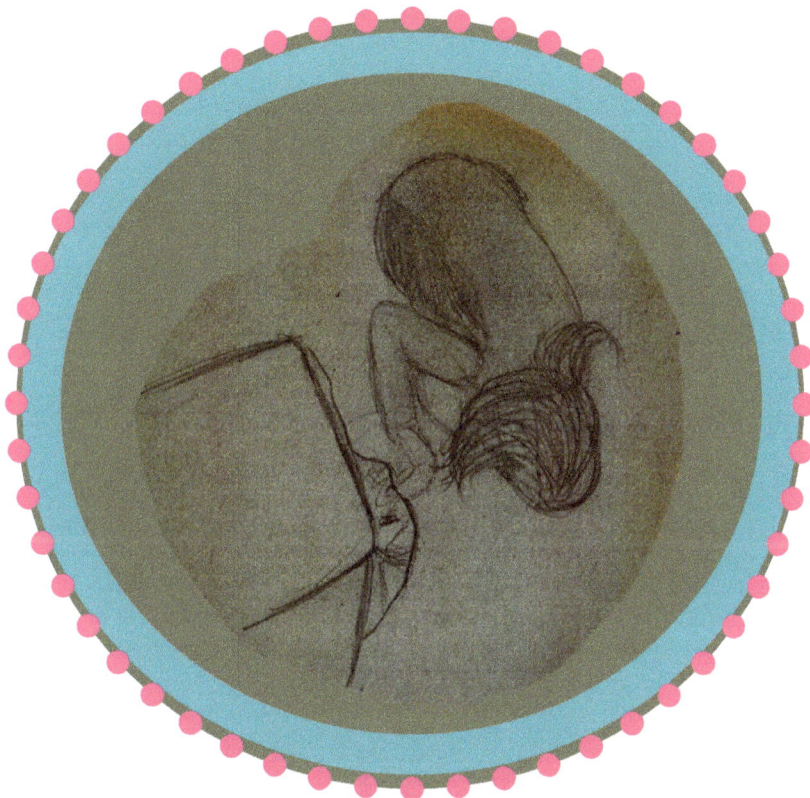

Mother looked for Wee Willie.
She looked near Wee Willie's small brush.
She looked near Wee Willie's small dish
and small bed. She looked near
Wee Willie's small coat.
She looked in every small place,
but Wee Willie was lost.

Mother telephoned the newspaper. "Someone may read about **Wee Willie** and telephone us," she said.

Mother telephoned the police station. "A policeman may see **Wee Willie** and telephone us," she said.

Mother telephoned the City Animal Shelter.
"Someone may find **Wee Willie**, and the lady at
the City Animal Shelter will telephone us," she said.

-12-

Mother telephoned the lady in the office
of the school. "The lady in the office will
telephone us if someone sees Wee Willie and
brings him to school," she said.

The telephone did not ring, and the children
did not stop crying.

That night Stanford wept in his bed, and
Elizabeth wept in her bed. Poor Wee Willie!
He would be hungry with no food. Poor Wee Willie!
He would be tired with no bed. Poor Wee Willie!
Poor Wee Willie! He would be sad and lonesome
with no friends to love and care for him.

-15-

The next day Stanford and Elizabeth cried.
They could not eat. They wept for poor Wee Willie.
Poor, poor Wee Willie!

The doorbell rang, and the children ran to the door. Stanford and Elizabeth were sad to see it was only the mailman, Mr. McCool.

Then they saw that Mr. McCool's coat was
open, and a wee, small head was looking out.
Mr. McCool said, "Did Wee Willie get lost?"
"Is this Wee Willie?"

The children were so thankful to see **Wee Willie**.
They were so thankful to have a
good friend like Mr. McCool.
"Thank you, thank you, Mr. McCool" they cried.
Wee Willie was so happy that he kissed
Stanford and Elizabeth and barked and jumped.

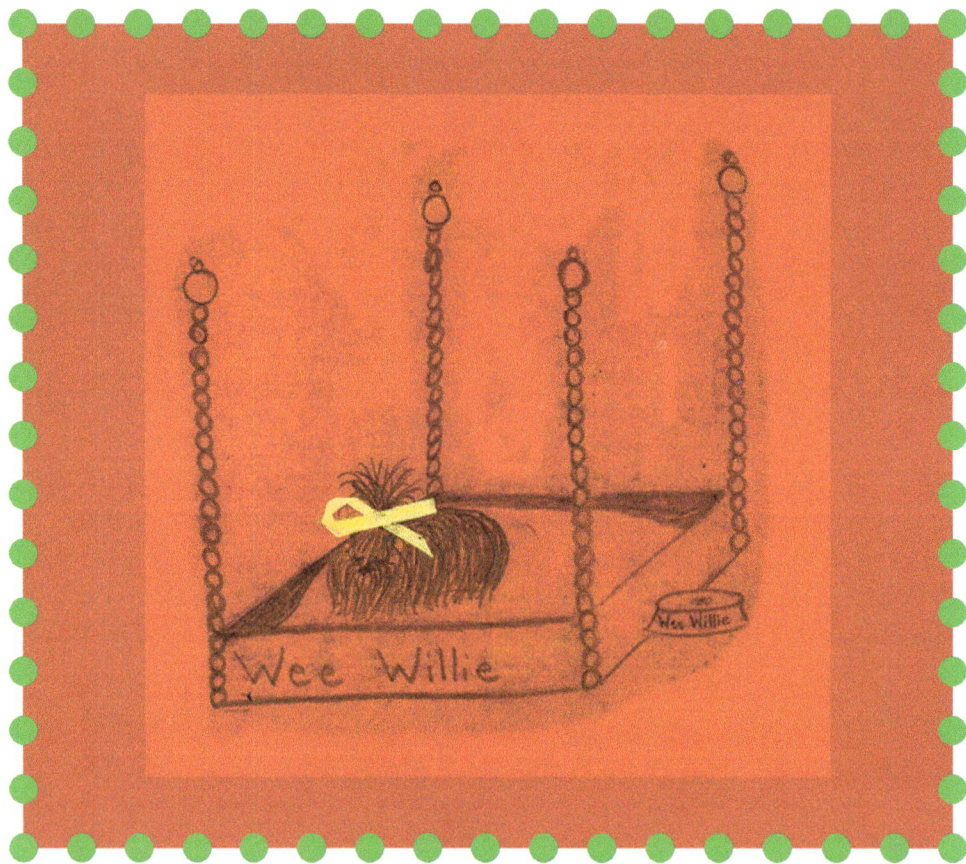

Everyone was thankful to have Wee Willie
at home again. Stanford and Elizabeth washed
and brushed Wee Willie. Mother put small pieces
of meat in the small dish for Wee Willie to eat.
Poor Wee Willie was so tired that he went to his
small bed and slept all day and all night.

That night Stanford and Elizabeth slept well too.
Everyone was thankful to have **Wee Willie** home.

Parent & Teacher
Help Kids with Reading Comprehension

1. Who is Wee Willie Winkie?

2. With whom does Wee Willie Winkie's live?

3. What does Wee Willie Winkie wear on cold days?

4. What three daily chores must be done if you own a dog?

5. Why did Stanford and Elizabeth start crying?

6. Whom did Mother call first?

7. Whom did Mother call second?

8. Whom did Mother call third?

9. Whom did Mother call fourth?

10. Why did Stanford and Elizabeth stop eating?

11. Who found Wee Willie Winkie?

12. What breed of dog is Wee Willie Winkie?

Answers:

1. A Dog   2. Standford and Elizabeth   3. Coat   4. Feed, Brush, and Walk

5. Lost Dog   6. Newspaper   7. Police Station   8. City Animal Shelter

9. School   10. Sad and Depressed   11. Mailman Mr. McCool   12. Yorkshire Terrier

Parent & Teacher
Help Kids Learn Math and Take Responsibility

Q. How many times do you have to feed and walk **Wee Willie Winkie** every day?

Q. How many times do you have to feed and walk **Wee Willie Winkie** every week?

My Daily Chores for Wee Willie Winkle

Monday	Feed/Walk	Brush	Feed/Walk	Play
Tuesday	Feed/Walk	Brush	Feed/Walk	Play
Wednesday	Feed/Walk	Brush	Feed/Walk	Play
Thursday	Feed/Walk	Brush	Feed/Walk	Play
Friday	Feed/Walk	Brush	Feed/Walk	Play
Saturday	Feed/Walk	Brush	Feed/Walk	Play
Sunday	Feed/Walk	Brush	Feed/Walk	Play

Answers: Every Day: 2   Every Week: 2x7 = 14

Never Give Up! Never Lose Hope!

Jacqueline Malman

www.ingramcontent.com/pod-product-compliance
Lightning Source LLC
Chambersburg PA
CBHW041559260326
41914CB00011B/1324

* 9 7 8 1 8 8 5 8 7 2 8 7 6 *